# How big is God?

Dave Hillis

Illustrations by
Nev Sandon

Tyndale House Publishers, Inc.
Wheaton, Illinois
Coverdale House Publishers Ltd.
London, England

All Scripture quotations in this
book are from *The Living Bible,*
© 1971 Tyndale House Publishers,
except for those identified as the
King James Version (KJV) or the
Twentieth Century New Testament
(TCNT).

Library of Congress Catalog
Card Number 74-80771
ISBN 8423-1510-1

Copyright © 1974 by
Dave Hillis, Wheaton, Illinois.
All rights reserved.

First printing, June 1974
Printed in the United States
of America

# How big is God?

This booklet is dedicated to those thousands of mothers and fathers whose sons and daughters serve the Lord Jesus on foreign fields.

# Contents

1. "Did anybody ever see God?" *1*
2. "What is God like?" *5*
3. "When did God begin?" *9*
4. "How many 'gods' are there, anyway?" *13*
5. "Where does God live?" *17*
6. "How strong is God, and what does he do?" *21*
7. "How big is God?" *25*
8. "How good is God?" *29*
9. "Did God make everything? Then who takes care of it?" *33*
10. "What if God ever changed his mind?" *37*
11. "Does God know everything?" *41*
12. "Did God really write the Bible?" *45*
13. "Why did God do miracles, anyway?" *49*
14. "Does God ever feel sad?" *53*
15. "Why does God love me?" *57*
16. "Does God really hear me when I pray?" *61*

17. "Does God really see everything?" *65*
18. "Why does a little voice inside me tell me what to do?" *69*
19. "Why did Jesus let himself be killed?" *73*
20. "If kids have to obey parents, shouldn't parents obey someone, too?" *77*
21. "God, I love you and I'll obey you, too!" *81*

# How big is God?

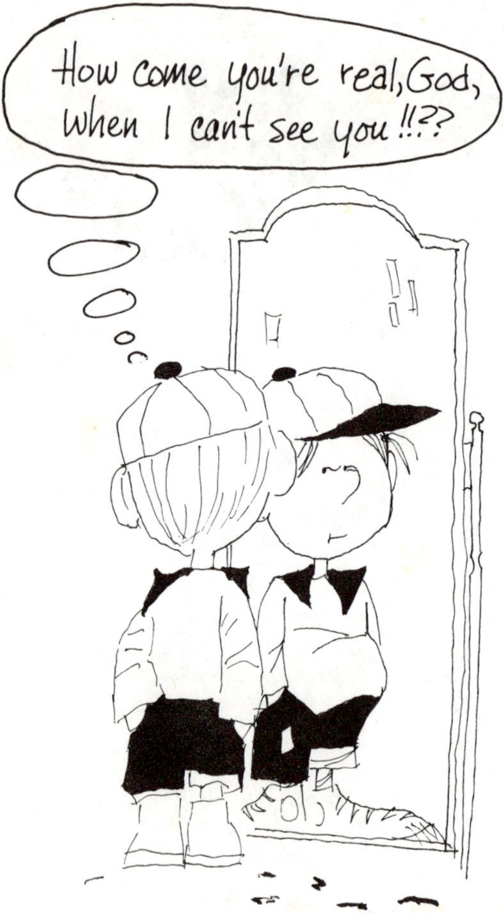
How come you're real, God, when I can't see you!!??

# 1

"Did anybody ever see God?"
*"Jesus did! And he's God, and men saw Jesus."*

"God is Spirit...."

"A spirit hath not flesh and bones...."

"No mere man has ever seen [God]...."

"... The unseen one who never dies; he alone is God...."

"No one has ever actually seen God, but, of course, his only Son has...."

"Christ is the exact likeness of the unseen God."

"Jesus replied, '... Anyone who has seen me has seen the Father!' "

"For in Christ there is all of God in a human body; *so you have everything when you have Christ....*"

*Jesus Christ is God's visible representation in the flesh.*

>John 4:24;  Luke 24:39 (KJV);
>1 Timothy 6:16;  1 Timothy 1:17;
>John 1:18;  Colossians 1:15a;  John 14:9;  Colossians 2:9, 10a.

Who are you, God ???

## 2. "What is God like?"

*"God is all powerful, perfectly holy, and very merciful!"*

"The Lord our God is one God."

"I am the Lord, the God of all mankind; is there anything too hard for me?"

"... God is light and in him is no darkness at all."

"I the Lord your God am holy...."

"... a gracious God, merciful, slow to get angry, and full of kindness. ..."

"O Lord, you are so good and kind, so ready to forgive; so full of mercy for all who ask your aid."

"... Love comes from God ... for God is love."

"... We know that God is always good and does only right. ..."

*Our God is one God, powerful, holy, and gracious.*

Deuteronomy 6:4 (KJV); Jeremiah 32:27; 1 John 1:5; Leviticus 19:2; Jonah 4:2; Psalm 86:5; 1 John 4:7, 8; 1 John 2:29.

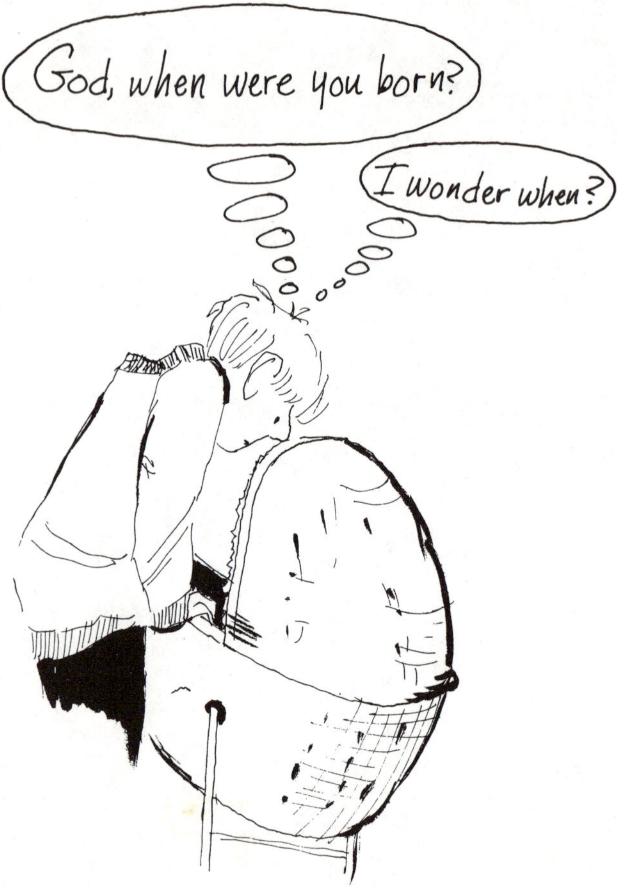
God, when were you born?
I wonder when?

## 3
"When did God begin?"
*"He didn't! He's without beginning or end!"*

"In the beginning God created the heaven and the earth."

"... You are God without beginning or end."

"Before anything else existed, there was Christ, with God. He has always been alive and is himself God."

"But you yourself [God] never grow old. You are forever, and your years never end."

" 'I am the A and the Z, the Beginning and the Ending of all things,' says God. . . ."

"God is so great that we cannot begin to know him. No one can begin to understand eternity."

*God is free from all laws of time for he is without beginning or end.*

Genesis 1:1a (KJV); Psalm 90:2b; John 1:1, 2; Psalm 102:27; Revelation 1:8; Job 36:26.

"My God's bigger than yours!"

## 4

"How many 'gods' are there, anyway?"

*"There are many false gods but only one true, triune God."*

"According to some people, there are a great many gods, both in heaven and on earth. But we know that there is only one God, the Father, who created all things ... and one Lord Jesus, who made everything and gives us life."

"Their gods are merely man-made things of silver and gold. They can't talk or see, despite their eyes and mouths! Nor can they hear, nor smell, nor use their hands or feet! Nor speak! And those who make and worship them are just as foolish as their idols are."

"What fools they are who carry around the wooden idols and pray to gods that cannot save!"

"There is salvation in no one else! Under all heaven there is no other name for men to call upon to save them."

"Before you Gentiles knew God you were slaves to so-called gods that did not even exist."

"I, the Lord your God, am very possessive. I will not share your affection with any other god!"

"If God is on our side, who can ever be against us? ... Who then will condemn us? Will Christ? *No!* For he is the one who died for us. ... The Holy Spirit prays for us. ..."

"Therefore go and make disciples in all the nations, baptizing them into the name of the Father and of the Son and of the Holy Spirit. ..."

*There are many false gods but only one true God.*

> 1 Corinthians 8:5, 6; Psalm 115:4–8; Isaiah 45:20b; Acts 4:12; Galatians 4:8; Exodus 20:5; Romans 8:31, 34, 26; Matthew 28:19.

Are you in here, God???

# 5

"Where does God live?"
*"He lives in heaven and in our hearts!"*

"God doesn't live in temples made by human hands. 'The heaven is my throne,' says the Lord through his prophets. ..."

"... I see the heavens opened and Jesus the Messiah standing beside God, at his right hand!"

"The high and lofty One ... inhabits eternity. ..."

"And I pray that Christ will be more and more at home in your hearts, living within you as you trust in him."

"He is the Holy Spirit, the Spirit who leads into all truth. ... Jesus replied, '... I will only reveal myself to those who love me and obey me. The Father will love them too, and we will come to them and live with them.'"

"Look! I have been standing at the door and I am constantly knocking. If anyone hears me calling him and opens the door, I will come in and fellowship with him and he with me."

Where is God? The Bible states that:

*God the Father is in heaven.*

*God the Son, Jesus Christ, is at the Father's right side—in heaven.*

*God the Holy Spirit lives in the hearts of all his people here on earth.*

> Acts 7:48, 49; Acts 7:56; Isaiah 57:15; Ephesians 3:17; John 14:17, 23; Revelation 3:20.

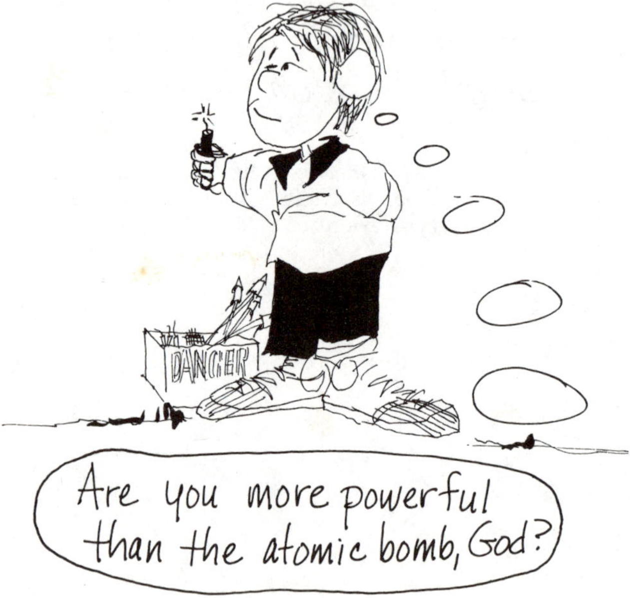
DANGER
Are you more powerful than the atomic bomb, God?

**6** "How strong is God, and what does he do?"
*"God's power is unlimited and he does mighty things to help us."*

"[God] was before all else began and it is his power that holds everything together."

"At the Flood, the Lord showed his control of all creation. Now he continues to unveil his power."

"He regulates the universe by the mighty power of his command."

"Your power and goodness, Lord, reach to the highest heavens. You have done such wonderful things."

"With God nothing shall be impossible."

"I know that you [God] can do anything and that no one can stop you."

"Nothing is too hard for you, O Lord God. ..."

"... You are the great and mighty God, the Lord of Hosts. You have all wisdom and do great and mighty miracles. ..."

"Because of [God's] great power he rules forever."

"I am the Almighty. ..."

"... Christ is the mighty power of God to save. ..."

"Yours is the mighty power and glory and victory and majesty. Everything in the heavens and earth is yours, O Lord, and this is your kingdom. We adore you as being in control of everything."

"He gives power to the tired and worn out, and strength to the weak."

*God's power is unlimited and he wants you to experience some of it.*

Colossians 1:17; Psalm 29:10; Hebrews 1:3; Psalm 71:19; Luke 1:37 (KJV); Job 42:2; Jeremiah 32:17, 18; Psalm 66:7a; Genesis 17:1; 1 Corinthians 1:24; 1 Chronicles 29:11; Isaiah 40:29.

"How come you're so big, God?"

# 7 "How big is God?"
*"God is everywhere, all the time."*

"Am I not everywhere in all of heaven and earth?"

"But is it possible that God would really live on earth? Why, even the skies and the highest heavens cannot contain you. ..."

"How great he is! His power is absolute! His understanding is unlimited."

"He does wonderful miracles, marvels without number."

"Canst thou by searching find out God? Canst thou find out the Almighty ... ?"

"His greatness is beyond discovery!"

"Your love and kindness are forever; your truth is as enduring as the heavens."

"God has put all things under his [Christ's] feet and made him the supreme Head of the church. ..."

"This is too glorious, too wonderful to believe! I can *never* be lost to your Spirit! I can *never* get away from my God! If I go up to heaven, you are there; if I go down to the place of the dead, you are there. If I ride the morning winds to the farthest oceans, even there your hand will guide me, your strength will support me. If I try to hide in the darkness, the night becomes light around me. For even darkness cannot hide from God; to you the night shines as bright as day. Darkness and light are both alike to you."

*God's greatness demonstrates his supreme position and absolute power.*

> Jeremiah 23:24b; 1 Kings 8:27; Psalm 147:5; Job 5:9; Job 11:7 (KJV); Psalm 145:3c; Psalm 89:2; Ephesians 1:22a; Psalm 139:6–12.

# 8 "How good is God?"
*"He is holy and therefore totally good."*

"Only God is truly good. . . ."

"God is good, and he loves goodness. . . ."

"The Lord is fair in everything he does, and full of kindness."

"God stands up to open heaven's court. He pronounces judgment. . . ."

"I am God and not man; I am the Holy One living among you. . . ."

"O God, your ways are holy."

"You love right and hate wrong; so God, even your God, has poured out more gladness upon you than on anyone else."

"Be holy now in everything you do, just as the Lord is holy, who invited you to be his child. He himself has said, 'You must be holy, for I am holy.'"

*God is perfect in his justice so he expects a respectful attitude.*

Luke 18:19; Psalm 11:7; Psalm 145:17; Psalm 82:1a; Hosea 11:9b; Psalm 77:13a; Hebrews 1:9; 1 Peter 1:15, 16.

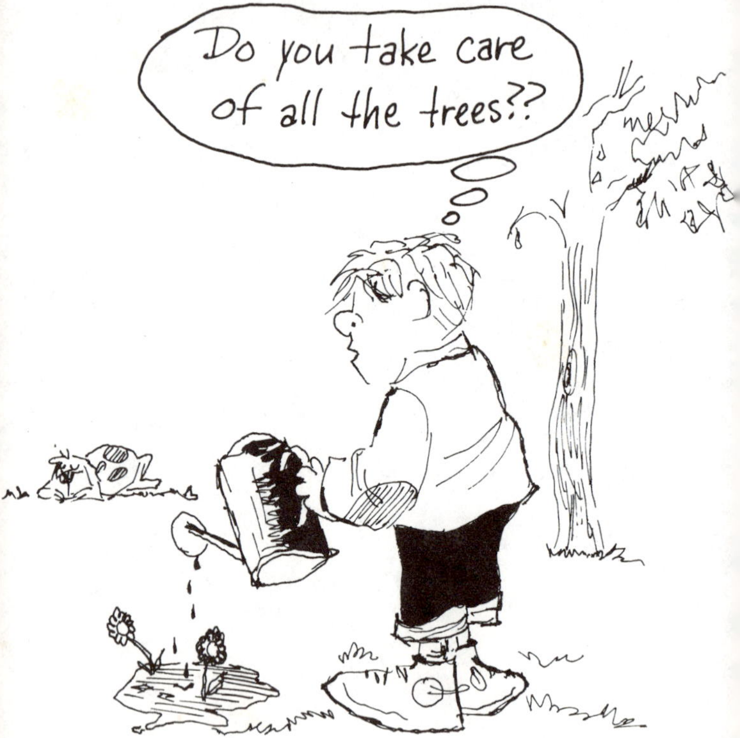
Do you take care of all the trees??

# 9

"Did God make everything? Then who takes care of it?"

*"God made everything and he takes care of it, too!"*

"Christ himself is the Creator who made everything in heaven and earth, the things we can see and the things we can't; the spirit world with its kings and kingdoms, its rulers and authorities; all were made by Christ for his own use and glory. He was before all else began and it is his power that holds everything together."

"He that built all things is God."

"He created everything there is—nothing exists that he didn't make."

"Day and night alike belong to you [God]; you made the starlight and the sun. All nature is within your hands. . . ."

"[God] formed the mountains by his mighty strength. He quiets the raging oceans and all the world's clamor."

". . . He gives his sunlight and . . . sends rain. . . ."

". . . the kind things he did such as sending you rain and good crops and giving you food. . . ."

"The Lord God formed from the soil every kind of animal and bird. ..."

"... the Lord God formed a man's body from the dust of the ground. ..."

"God made man like his Maker. Like God did God make man. Man and maid did he make them."

*God not only created everything—he takes care of it, too.*

> Colossians 1:16, 17; Hebrews 3:4 (KJV); John 1:3; Psalm 74:16, 17; Psalm 65:6, 7; Matthew 5:45; Acts 14:17; Genesis 2:19; Genesis 2:7; Genesis 1:27.

Aren't you ever wrong, God?

## 10. "What if God ever changed his mind?" *"God can't change his mind, so he can't be wrong."*

"I am the Lord—I do not change."

"What a God he is! How perfect in every way! All his promises prove true."

"You [God] yourself will never change, and your years will never end."

"... God is never subject to change...."

". . . your Father in heaven is perfect."

". . . you are the God who always does what is right."

"He is the Rock. His work is perfect. Everything he does is just and fair. He is faithful, without sin."

"All [God] does is just and good, and all his laws are right, for they are formed from truth and goodness, and stand firm forever."

"The Lord is coming to judge the earth; he will judge the nations fairly and with truth!"

"[God] shows how to distinguish right from wrong, how to find the right decision every time."

"God also bound himself with an oath, so that those he promised to help would be perfectly sure and never need to wonder whether he might change his plans."

"O Lord, you have reigned from prehistoric times, from the everlasting past. ... Your royal decrees cannot be changed. Holiness is forever the keynote of your reign."

*God is perfect in every way and never wrong ... and he still loves you!*

Malachi 3:6; Psalm 18:30a; Hebrews 1:12b; James 1:17 (TCNT); Matthew 5:48b; Psalm 31:1b; Deuteronomy 32:4; Psalm 111:7, 8; Psalm 96:13; Proverbs 2:9; Hebrews 6:17; Psalm 93:2, 5.

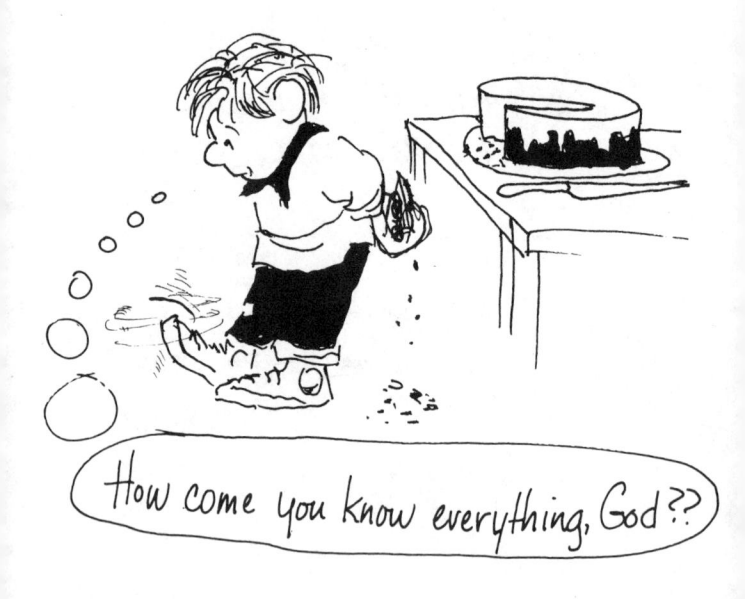
How come you know everything, God??

# 11 "Does God know everything?" "*Yes, God knows everything.*"

"The Lord's wisdom founded the earth; his understanding established all the universe and space."

"The depths of hell are open to God's knowledge. How much more the hearts of all mankind!"

"Now we understand that you [Jesus] know everything and don't need anyone to tell you anything."

"Oh, what a wonderful God we have! How great are his wisdom and knowledge and riches! How impossible it is for us to understand his decisions and his methods!"

"The Spirit of the Lord shall rest upon [Christ], the Spirit of wisdom, understanding, counsel and might; the Spirit of knowledge and of the fear of the Lord."

"Woe to those who try to hide their plans from God, who try to keep him in the dark concerning what they do!"

"In [Christ] lie hidden all the mighty, untapped treasures of wisdom and knowledge."

*God does know everything, even things we try to hide.*

Proverbs 3:19; Proverbs 15:11; John 16:30; Romans 11:33; Isaiah 11:2; Isaiah 29:15; Colossians 2:3.

Did you really write this book?

# 12

"Did God really write the Bible?"
*"The Word of God was written by men of God under the direction of the Spirit of God."*

"The whole Bible was given to us by inspiration from God and is useful to teach us what is true and to make us realize what is wrong in our lives; it straightens us out and helps us to do what is right."

"... the Scripture, which cannot be untrue...."

"There is utter truth in all your laws; your decrees are eternal."

"Forever, O Lord, your Word stands firm in heaven."

"Heaven and earth shall disappear, but my words stand sure forever."

"We have seen and proved that what the prophets said came true.... For no prophecy recorded in Scripture was ever thought up by the prophet himself. It was the Holy Spirit within these godly men who gave them true messages from God."

"They hardened their hearts like flint, afraid to hear the words that God, the Lord of Hosts, commanded them—the laws he had revealed to them by his Spirit through the early prophets."

*The Word of God was written by men of God under the direction of the Spirit of God.*

> 2 Timothy 3:16;  John 10:35;
> Psalm 119:160;  Psalm 119:89;
> 2 Peter 1:19, 21;  Zechariah 7:12.

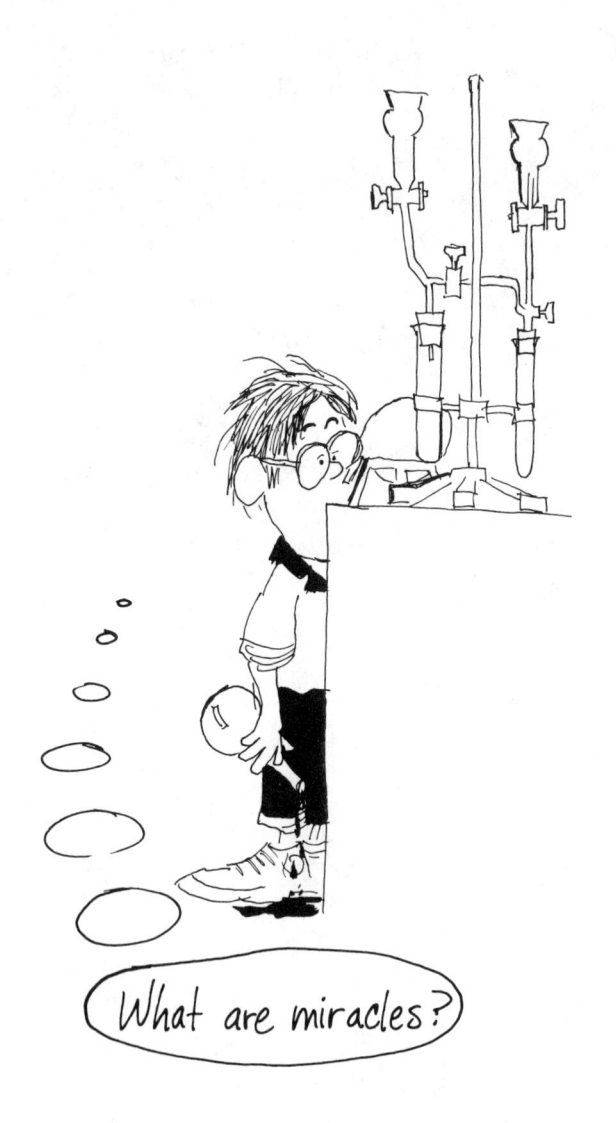
What are miracles?

# 13

"Why did God do miracles, anyway?"
*"Miracles are mighty acts of God to help people believe in him."*

"His miracles demonstrate his honor, majesty, and eternal goodness."

"Where among the heathen gods is there a god like you? Where are their miracles?"

"Your mighty miracles give proof that you care."

"Then fire from God flashed down from heaven and burned up the young bull, the wood, stones, the dust, and even evaporated all the water. . . . And when the people saw it, they fell to their faces upon the ground shouting, 'Jehovah is God!' . . ."

"Jesus' disciples saw him do many other miracles besides the ones told about in this book; but these are recorded so that you will believe that he is the . . . Son of God. . . ."

". . . the miracles I do; these have been assigned me by the Father, and they prove that the Father has sent me."

"[Jesus] began to pour out his denunciations against the cities where he had done most of his miracles, because they hadn't turned to God."

*Miracles are supernatural exhibitions by God in our physical world.*

> Psalm 111:3; Psalm 86:8; Psalm 75:1b; 1 Kings 18:38, 39; John 20:30, 31; John 5:36; Matthew 11:20.

Do you ever feel "hurt," God?

## 14

"Does God ever feel sad?"

*"God is 'hurt' by man's pride and disobedience."*

"Oh, that my people would listen to me! Oh, that Israel would follow me. ..."

"I don't want your sacrifices—I want your love; I don't want your offerings—I want you to know me."

"It isn't sacrifices and offering which you really want from your people. Burnt animals bring no special joy to your heart. But you have accepted the offer of my lifelong service."

"They rebelled against him and grieved his Holy Spirit."

"Oh, how often they rebelled against him in those years and grieved his heart."

"When the Lord God saw the extent of human wickedness ... he was sorry he had made them. It broke his heart."

" 'But,' God says, 'I was very angry with them, for their hearts were always looking somewhere else instead of up to me, and they never found the paths I wanted them to follow.' "

"Don't cause the Holy Spirit sorrow by the way you live."

*God is "hurt" by man's pride and disobedience.*

Psalm 81:13; Hosea 6:6; Psalm 40:6; Isaiah 63:10; Psalm 78:40; Genesis 6:5; Hebrews 3:10; Ephesians 4:30a.

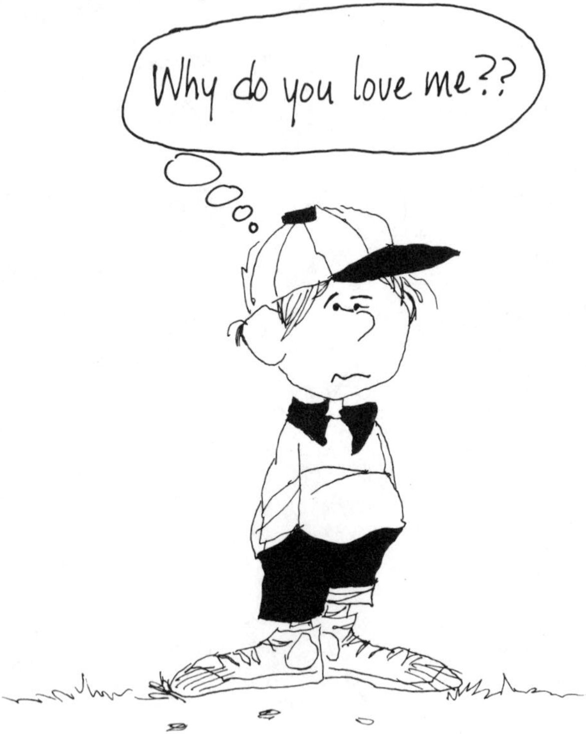
Why do you love me??

# 15 "Why does God love me?"
## *"Because he is love."*

"I see myself so stupid and so ignorant; I must seem like an animal to you, O God. But even so, you love me!"

"My God is changeless in his love for me and he will come and help me."

"For [God] loves us dearly, and his truth endures."

"Jesus replied, '... I will only reveal myself to those who love me and obey me.'"

"... The greatest love is shown when a person lays down his life for his friends; and you are my friends if you obey me."

"... May you be able to feel and understand, as all God's children should, how long, how wide, how deep, and how high his love really is; and to experience this love for yourselves. ..."

"... Nothing can ever separate us from his love. Death can't, and life can't. The angels won't, and all the powers of hell itself cannot keep God's love away."

"... God showed his great love for us by sending Christ to die for us while we were still sinners."

"... We see what real love is: it is not our love for God, but his love for us when he sent his Son to satisfy God's anger against our sins."

*God loves us because he is love, not because we deserve it or earn it in any way.*

Psalm 73:22, 23; Psalm 59:10a; Psalm 117:2a; John 14:23; John 15:13, 14; Ephesians 3:18, 19; Romans 8:38; Romans 5:8; 1 John 4:10.

"Hey, thanks for answering my prayer, God!!!"

## 16

"Does God really hear me when I pray?"
*"Yes, God hears us when we pray, and he answers, too!"*

"Each morning I will look to you [God] in heaven and lay my requests before you, praying earnestly."

"The earnest prayer of a righteous man has great power and wonderful results."

"The Lord is far from the wicked, but he hears the prayers of the righteous."

"Therefore he will listen to me and answer when I call to him."

"One day Jesus told his disciples a story to illustrate their need for constant prayer and to show them that they must keep praying until the answer comes."

"Pray all the time. Ask God for anything in line with the Holy Spirit's wishes."

"If you want to know what God wants you to do, ask him, and he will gladly tell you, for he is always ready to give a bountiful supply of wisdom to all who ask him. ..."

"Don't recite the same prayer over and over. ... Your Father knows exactly what you need. ..."

"Don't be weary in prayer; keep at it; watch for God's answers and remember to be thankful when they come."

"Don't worry about anything; instead, pray about everything; tell God your needs and don't forget to thank him for his answers."

*Prayer is communication between man and God. God's answer might be "Yes," "No," or "Wait."*

Psalm 5:3; James 5:16b; Proverbs 15:29; Psalm 4:3b; Luke 18:1; Ephesians 6:18a; James 1:5; Matthew 6:7, 8; Colossians 4:2; Philippians 4:6.

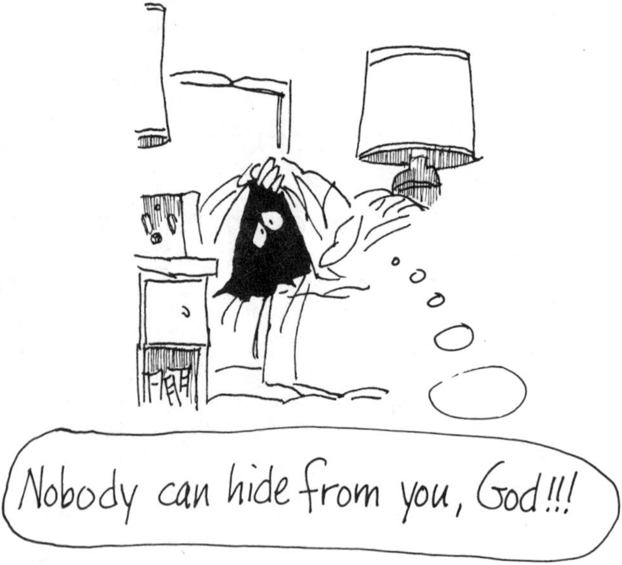
Nobody can hide from you, God!!!

# 17 "Does God really see everything?" *"Yes, God sees everything!"*

"The Lord is watching everywhere and keeps his eye on both the evil and the good."

"He watches every movement of the nations. O rebel lands, he will deflate your pride."

"He knows about everyone, everywhere. Everything about us is bare and wide open to the all-seeing eyes of our living God; nothing can be hidden from him to whom we must explain all that we have done."

"Fools! Is God deaf and blind —he who makes ears and eyes? ... He knows everything—doesn't he also know what you are doing?"

"... Your eyes are open to all the ways of men, and you reward everyone according to his life and deeds."

"Am I a God who is only in one place and cannot see what they are doing? Can anyone hide from me?"

"You spread out our sins before you—our secret sins— and see them all."

*God's "eyesight" is perfect. He sees everything.*

Proverbs 15:3; Psalm 66:7b; Hebrews 4:13; Psalm 94:8–10; Jeremiah 32:19b; Jeremiah 23:23, 24a; Psalm 90:8.

How come I "hurt" when I do wrong??

# 18

"Why does a little voice inside me tell me what to do?" *"Because God has given you a conscience to help you do right."*

"For the truth about God is known to them instinctively; God has put this knowledge in their hearts."

"[God] will punish the heathen when they sin, even though they never had God's written laws, for down in their hearts they know right from wrong ... their own conscience accuses them or sometimes excuses them. ..."

"Obey the laws, then, for two reasons: first, to keep from being punished, and second, just because you know you should."

"Some people have disobeyed their consciences and have deliberately done what they knew was wrong."

"These [false] teachers will tell lies with straight faces and do it so often that their consciences won't even bother them."

"I will put my laws in their hearts so that they will want to obey them."

"A man's conscience is the Lord's searchlight exposing his hidden motives."

*Your conscience is a God-given sin detector for you.*

> Romans 1:19; Romans 2:14, 15; Romans 13:5; 1 Timothy 1:19b; 1 Timothy 4:2; Hebrews 10:16b; Proverbs 20:27.

"If Jesus was so good why did they kill him??"

# 19 "Why did Jesus let himself be killed?"
*"He died to pay the penalty for our sin."*

"[Christ] laid aside his mighty power and glory, taking the disguise of a slave and becoming like men. And he humbled himself even further, going as far as actually to die a criminal's death on a cross."

"For I must die just as was prophesied. . . ."

" 'Am I some dangerous criminal,' [Jesus] asked, 'that

you had to arm yourselves with swords and clubs before you could arrest me? ... But this is all happening to fulfill the words of the prophets as recorded in the Scriptures.' "

"No one can kill me without my consent—I lay down my life voluntarily. For I have the right and power to lay it down when I want to and also the right and power to take it again."

"Christ ... died once for the sins of all us guilty sinners, although he himself was innocent of any sin at any time, that he might bring us safely home to God."

*Jesus gave up his life so that we might have eternal life. His death paid our sin's penalty, giving us a pardon.*

Philippians 2:7, 8; Matthew 26:24a; Matthew 26:55, 56; John 10:18; 1 Peter 3:18.

Be careful, Mom, God doesn't want you to get mad!!!

## 20

"If kids have to obey parents, shouldn't parents obey someone, too?"
*"Yes, parents ought to obey God."*

"The character of even a child can be known by the way he acts—whether what he does is pure and right."

"Only a fool despises his father's advice; a wise son considers each suggestion."

"You children must always obey your fathers and mothers, for that pleases the

77

Lord. Fathers, don't scold your children so much that they become discouraged and quit trying."

"Children, obey your parents; this is the right thing to do because God has placed them in authority over you. Honor your father and mother."

"Teach a child to choose the right path, and when he is older he will remain upon it."

"Don't fail to correct your children; discipline won't hurt them! They won't die if you use a stick on them!"

"If you refuse to discipline your son, it proves you don't love him; for if you love him you will be prompt to punish him."

"Discipline your son in his early years while there is hope. If you don't you will ruin his life."

"Don't keep on scolding and nagging your children, making them angry and resentful.... Bring them up with the loving discipline the Lord himself approves, with suggestions and godly advice."

"Scolding and spanking a child helps him to learn. Left to himself, he brings shame to his mother."

*Parents are responsible to God for giving the correct attention to discipline of their children.*

Proverbs 20:11; Proverbs 15:5; Colossians 3:20, 21; Ephesians 6:1, 2a; Proverbs 22:6; Proverbs 23:13, 14b; Proverbs 13:24; Proverbs 19:18; Ephesians 6:4; Proverbs 29:15.

# 21

"God, I love you and I'll obey you, too!"
*"We prove our love for God in our obedience and faithfulness to him."*

"You must love the Lord your God and obey every one of his commands."

"Oh, love the Lord, all of you who are his people; for the Lord protects those who are loyal to him, but harshly punishes all who haughtily reject him."

"You must love the Lord your God with all your heart, and with all your soul, and with all your strength, and with all your mind. And you must love your neighbor just as much as you love yourself."

"If you love me, obey me. . . ."

"Obey God because you are his children; don't slip back into your old ways—doing evil because you knew no better."

"If anyone says 'I love God,' but keeps on hating his brother, he is a liar. . . ."

"So you see, our love for him comes as a result of his loving us first."

"God is more pleased when

we are just and fair than when we give him gifts."

"Obedience is far better than sacrifice. He is much more interested in your listening to him than in your offering the fat of rams to him."

"To do right honors God; to sin is to despise him."

"God blesses those who obey him; happy is the man who puts his trust in the Lord."

"The Lord loves those who hate evil; he protects the lives of his people, and rescues them from the wicked. Light is sown for the godly and joy for the good. May all who are godly be happy in the Lord and crown him, our holy God."

*People demonstrate their love for God through obedience and faithfulness.*

Deuteronomy 11:1; Psalm 31:23; Luke 10:27; John 14:15; 1 Peter 1:14; 1 John 4:20; 1 John 4:19; Proverbs 21:3; 1 Samuel 15:22b; Proverbs 14:2; Proverbs 16:20; Psalm 97:10–12.